Rocky Mountain ALPINE FLOWERS

MARLENE M. BORNEMAN

The Colorado Mountain Club Press
Golden, Colorado

Rocky Mountain Alpine Flowers
© 2019 by The Colorado Mountain Club

All rights reserved. No part of this publication may be reproduced or transmitted in any form or by any means, electronic or mechanical, including photocopy, recording, or by any information storage and retrieval system, without permission in writing from the publisher.

PUBLISHED BY

The Colorado Mountain Club Press
710 Tenth Street, Suite 200, Golden, Colorado 80401
303-996-2743   e-mail: cmcpress@cmc.org

Founded in 1912, The Colorado Mountain Club is the largest outdoor recreation, education, and conservation organization in the Rocky Mountains. Look for our books at your local bookstore or outdoor retailer or online at www.cmc.org/store.

    Marlene M. Borneman: author, photographer
    Clyde Soles: publisher
    Erika K. Arroyo: design, composition, and production

CONTACTING THE PUBLISHER
We greatly appreciate when readers alert us to errors or outdated information by contacting us at cmcpress@cmc.org.

DISTRIBUTED TO THE BOOK TRADE BY
The Mountaineers Books, 1001 SW Klickitat Way, Suite 201, Seattle, WA 98134, 800-553-4453, www.mountaineersbooks.org

COVER PHOTO: Old Man of the Mountain and the Mummy Range, Rocky Mountain National Park. Marlene Borneman

We gratefully acknowledge the financial support of the people of Colorado through the Scientific and Cultural Facilities District of greater Denver for our publishing activities.

ISBN: 978-1937052706

Printed in Korea

CONTENTS

Introduction 9
Using This Pack Guide 12

WHITE/CREAM/GREEN FLOWERS

Gray's angelica 16
Alpine dusty maiden 17
Alpine thistle (mountain thistle) 18
Blackhead daisy 19
Coulter's daisy 20
Yarrow 21
American false candytuft 22
Wild candytuft (mountain candytuft, alpine pennycress) 23
Alpine sandwort (alpine stitchwort) 24
Fendler's sandwort 25
Long-stalked starwort 26
Mouse-ear chickweed 27
Rocky mountain nailwort 28
Arctic gentian 29
Alp-lily 30
Mountain death camas (wand lily) 31
Alpine spring beauty (big-rooted spring beauty) .. 32
Hooded lady's tresses 33
White bog orchid (scentbottle orchid) 34
Parry's lousewort 35
Fringed grass-of-parnassus 36
Snowlover (rocky mountain snowlover) 37
Alpine phlox 38
Brandegee's sky pilot (honey sky pilot or polemonium) ... 39
Globe gilia (Hoosier Pass ipomopsis) 40

Alpine bistort	41
Alpine mountain sorrel	42
American bistort	43
Subalpine sulfur flower	44
Pygmy-flower rock jasmine (northern fairy candelabra)	45
Rock jasmine (sweet-flower rock jasmine)	46
Globeflower	47
Marsh marigold	48
Narcissus anemone	49
Mountain dryad (mountain avens)	0
Alpine willow (rock willow)	50
Snow willow	51
Dotted saxifrage	52
Front range alumroot (Hall's alumroot)	53
Nodding saxifrage	54
Rocky mountain alumroot (bracted alumroot)	55
Side-flowered mitrewort (white mitrewort)	56
Snowball saxifrage (diamond-leaf saxifrage)	57
Weak saxifrage (pygmy saxifrage)	58
Sharpleaf valerian	59

YELLOW/ORANGE FLOWERS

Alpine Parsley	62
Alpine sagewort (dwarf sagewort)	63
Arrowleaf ragwort	64
Black-tip ragwort	65
Broadleaf arnica	66
Colorado ragwort	67
Dwarf mountain ragwort (Fremont's ragwort)	68
Hoary groundsel (Werner's groundsel, rock groundsel)	69
Holm's ragwort	70
Mt. Albert goldenrod (dwarf goldenrod)	71
Nodding Ragwort	72

Old man of the mountain (alpine sunflower)............73
Orange agoseris (orange mountain dandelion)..........74
Pale agoseris, (mountain dandelion)...................75
Parry's arnica (rayless arnica).......................76
Pygmy goldenweed (small sunspot).....................77
Saffron ragwort......................................78
Showy alpine ragwort.................................79
Stemless four-nerve daisy (goldflower)...............80
Alpine twinpod.......................................81
Alpine wallflower (western wallflower)...............82
Golden draba...83
Thick draba..84
Yellow stonecrop.....................................85
Avalanche lily (glacier lily)........................86
Alpine paintbrush (shortflower Indian paintbrush)....87
Fern leaf lousewort (bracted or Payson's lousewort)..88
Western yellow paintbrush............................89
Alpine poppy (arctic poppy, kluane poppy)............90
Subalpine monkeyflower...............................91
Alpine golden buckwheat..............................92
Eschscholtz's buttercup (subalpine buttercup)........93
Rocky mountain buttercup (Macauley's buttercup)......94
Snow buttercup (alpine buttercup)....................95
Alpine avens...96
Alpine ivesia..97
Sibbaldia (creeping sibbaldia, cloverleaf rose)......98
Golden saxifrage (goldbloom saxifrage)...............99
Little-leaf alumroot (common alumroot)..............100
Whiplash saxifrage..................................101
Arctic yellow violet................................102

RED/PINK FLOWERS
Glacier daisy (subalpine daisy).....................104
Tall daisy (tall fleabane, beautiful daisy).........105

Moss campion 106
King's crown 107
Queen's crown (rose crown) 108
Alpine clover 109
Dwarf clover 110
Parry's clover 111
Alpine laurel 112
Fitweed (Case's corydalis) 113
Pygmy bitterroot (alpine lewsia) 114
Hornemann's willowherb 115
Alpine lousewort (sudetic lousewort) 116
Elephant's head 117
Split-leaf Indian paintbrush (rosy paintbrush) 118
Dense-flowered dock (alpine dock) 119
Alpine primrose (fairy primrose) 120
Parry's primrose 121
James' false saxifrage (rock saxifrage) 122

BLUE/PURPLE FLOWERS
Pinnate-leaf daisy 124
Alpine bluebells 125
Alpine forget-me-not 126
Purple fringe (silky phacelia) 127
Tall chiming bells (streamside bluebells, fringed
   bluebells) 128
Arctic bellflower (alpine harebell) 129
Fringed gentian 130
Little gentian (northern gentian, autumn dwarf
   gentian) 131
Moss gentian (pygmy gentian) 132
Parry's gentian 133
Perennial fringed gentian 134
Star gentian 135
Alpine kittentail 136

American alpine speedwell	137
Clustered penstemon	138
Hall's beardtongue	139
Whipple's penstemon	140
Jacob's ladder	141
Sky pilot	142
Alpine columbine (dwarf columbine, rocky mountain blue columbine)	143
Colorado blue columbine	144
Columbian monkshood	145
Subalpine larkspur	146
Mountain blue violet (hook-spurred violet)	147
Glossary	148
References and Resources	151
Index	152

Sky Pilot on Sunshine Peak, San Juan Range.

*For my grandchildren,
Learn, Grow, and Thrive.*

Parry's Primrose in the San Juan Mountains.

INTRODUCTION

Welcome to the unique and extraordinary world of the alpine tundra of the Rocky Mountains.

Alpine is synonymous with "high mountains and high altitude," approximately any area above 11,500 feet in the southern Rockies. The alpine life zone is absent of trees, but abundant with beautiful miniature plants and minimalist animals. For the purpose of this pack guide, tundra is an area with its own ecosystem (a community of organisms interacting with their physical environment) within the alpine life zone. Only certain plants have adapted to the alpine tundra. Many of the alpine plants and subalpine plants crossover life zones boundaries; therefore, subalpine species are included in this pack guide.

Little has changed in Colorado's alpine tundra since Ann Zwinger and Beatrice "Betty" Willard researched and recorded findings in the early 1970s, which led to writing *Land Above The Trees*. The tundra plants are as fascinating now as they were then. These miniature plants, some only inches high or less, are characterized as hardy, resilient, survivors and beautiful treasures among the plant world.

At first sight the alpine tundra may appear as a barren and hostile environment. Spend time up in the thin air looking closer and you will find an exquisite and complex plant system. Note that Colorado has the largest scope of alpine tundra in the continental United States.

Plants that call the alpine tundra home have developed specialized adaptations to cope with challenges of the harsh environment above 11,500 feet. They experience a very short growing season, severe winds/storms, low temperatures, and often drought conditions. So how do they not only survive but also thrive in such an environment? You will notice most of these plants grow close to the ground allowing the strong storms and winds to simply blow over them not blow them down. A majority of the plants have deep taproots spreading out to help find water and keep them firmly secured to the thin soil. Many of the alpine and subalpine plants are covered with hairs, either/or on the leaves, stems, and flowers to help trap heat and moisture and act as a sunscreen. Look at the Alpine Sunflower, a.k.a. Old Man of the Mountain; it always faces east to the sun, avoiding strong winds from the west and taking advantage of the warmth of the sun.

Like any area that we may live, the alpine consists of diverse communities; each with their own characteristics; each in close proximately complementing each other. Here is a brief description of the alpine tundra communities.

FELLFIELD COMMUNITIES

A fellfield can be described as a field of stones on tundra slopes, where winds seem to always be present. Fellfields are characterized as dry, rocky areas. It is here you will find the tiniest of plants catching on thin soils that have blow between rocks. Cushion plants, less than a couple of inches high like to plant their feet here.

SNOWBEDS

An area where snow persists very late into summer and often remains wet throughout the summer. Hardy plants found here bloom late in the summer. Here you will find plants that grow and reproduce in a very short time span and can even start growth under snow cover.

BOULDER FIELDS

As the name implies, this area consists of large boulders strewn over each other. Lichens like to grow here on the large surfaces of boulders, but there are pockets of dirt blown in between and warmed by the sun, where water get traps providing the perfect flower garden. Boulders that overhang each other provide shelter supporting plant life.

TALUS AND SCREE SLOPES

A steep slope where the large boulder fields have weathered down to smaller gravel is called scree or talus. Many plants find a home in between the warm scree where their root system can actually help stabilize this ever-moving rocky slope.

ALPINE MEADOWS

Taller plants grow in alpine meadows where they are sheltered by rolling dips in the tundra and less wind than fellfields, scree slopes, and boulder fields. Flowers have more soil here and room to spread out and flourish, often with large patches of flowers. Grasses and sedges fill in adding richness to the soil. Blooming time in the alpine meadows is mid-summer.

ALPINE MARSH

Yes, there are marshes and bogs in the alpine/subalpine zones! These marshes are situated along a flattening slope or on the bottom of a mountainside where melting snow or a spring is constantly feeding the ground, sometimes resulting in small tarns or rivulets. Wet and cold are comfortable and necessary elements for these plants.

The majority of plants are very picky about where they put down roots. Soil types, variations in elevations, light, winds, and moisture all decide what plants grow where including the alpine tundra.

Delight in, appreciate, and learn with your time in this part of Colorado's world—the alpine tundra!

Alpine Twinpod, Mosquito Range.

USING THIS PACK GUIDE

It is hard to miss the brilliant displays of Rocky Mountain wildflowers! Do you ever wonder what the names are of the flowers that you may see on trails and roadsides? You do not need to be a botanist to learn to use botany and enjoy the fascinating world of wildflowers. This wildflower pack guide is designed for the novice to the seasoned wildflower enthusiast to identify and get to know Colorado's common, not so common, and rare wildflowers.

COLOR GROUPS

This pack guide is organized by color. This is a quick and easy approach to the identification of flowers. Turn to the color section that best matches the flower you want to identify. Keep in mind there are variations to flower color and structure. For example, a flower that is traditionally red may have pink or white variations due to hybridizing or environmental factors. You may need to check several color sections.

COMMON NAMES

Common names are listed for each flower. Common names are a result of regions and generations. There is no standardization for common names and one flower can have several common names. I have made every effort to select the most-used common name for the Rocky Mountain Region. For some flowers more than one common name is listed.

SCIENTIFIC NAMES

Because using common names can lead to miscommunication and confusion, it is best to learn the scientific names (genus and species). For some plants, synonyms are given due to differences with botanists various works and findings. Taxonomy is a rapidly changing science and constantly evolving so systems of naming and classifying plants will not be in agreement.

PLANT FAMILIES

Plant families are listed alphabetically within each color section. Plants are classified into family groups. Traditionally, classification of flowering plants was based on flower structure. There have been many changes recently in classification of flowering families and species due to genetic research and evidence. As a result some species have been moved from one family to another. This pack guide reflects the most up to date floras.

LIFE ZONES

Plants grow in degrees of elevations called Life Zones. Note that environmental differences and changes affect species, so plants will cross life zones.

Colorado has five life zones:
- Plains: 3,315 ft. – 5,600 ft.
- Foothills: 5,600 ft. – 8,000 ft.
- Montane: 8,000 ft. – 10,500 ft.
- Sub-alpine: 10,500 ft. – 11, 500 ft.
- Alpine: 11,500 ft. – 14, 431 ft. (Mount Elbert the highest point in Colorado)

HABITATS

Habitats are listed for each plant. From prairies to tundra, Colorado has a diversity of habitats lending to a tremendous diversity of wildflowers. Knowing where a flower likes to plant its feet helps with locating the flower and with the correct identification.

LOOK FOR

Under this section the characteristics of the flower; height, leaf shape, and general flower structure are given. Any unique identifying characteristics of the flower are also provided. A 10x hand lens is recommended to closely examine hairs, markings etc.

BLOOM

This section provides the most likely time to find the greatest numbers of the flower in bloom. Be aware there are several variables to blooming times: seasonal temperatures, precipitation (including the year's snowpack), storms/winds, and changing soil conditions.

This pack guide is meant to be part of your hiking gear when you are heading out on Colorado's trails. You may want to add a hand lens, pen, notepad, and camera. It is my hope to spark or further your interest in knowing and loving Colorado's wildflowers. For more information consult a field guide with dichotomous keys in continuing to expand your knowledge of wildflowers. We welcome any corrections, suggestions and additions.

When in Colorado's outdoors please follow Leave No Trace ethics. Do not pick or try to transplant wildflowers. Simply enjoy their beauty in the wild and leave them for others. In addition, many pollinators and other animals depend on wildflowers for food and/or shelter. In preserving Colorado's native wildflowers you help preserve our native pollinators.

Glacier Daisies, Wild Basin, Rocky Mountain National Park.

White • Cream • Green Flowers

American bistort.

White/Cream/Green Flowers

GRAY'S ANGELICA
Angelica grayi
Parsley Family (Apiaceae)

LIFE ZONE: Montane, subalpine, alpine
HABITAT: Moist forest, high meadows, tundra
HEIGHT: 6" - 12" in the alpine, up to 24" in lower elevations
LOOK FOR: Rough, egg-shaped-lanceolate leaves, divided into three leaflets with toothed margins on a stout stem. Tiny greenish-white flowers arranged in ball-like clusters on umbels.
BLOOM: Summer

ALPINE DUSTY MAIDEN
Chaenactis douglasii var. *alpina*
Sunflower Family (Asteraceae)

White/Cream/Green Flowers

LIFE ZONE: Subalpine, alpine
HABITAT: Scree slopes, gravelly soils
HEIGHT: 3" - 5"
LOOK FOR: Dusty green, fern-like, finely cut leaves forming a low mound. White-pinkish disk flowers on short stems.
BLOOM: Summer

White/Cream/Green Flowers

ALPINE THISTLE
(MOUNTAIN THISTLE)
Cirsium scopulorum
Sunflower Family (Asteraceae)

LIFE ZONE: Subalpine, alpine
HABITAT: Open alpine meadows, scree slopes
HEIGHT: 12" - 60"
LOOK FOR: Bright green narrow spiny leaves, fine white woolly hairs underneath, smooth or slightly hairy on top, alternate on stem. Crowded clusters of woolly disk flowers varying colors from white, yellow, purple, or pink on a stout stem.
BLOOM: Summer-autumn

BLACKHEAD DAISY
Erigeron melanocephalus
Sunflower Family (Asteraceae)

White/Cream/Green Flowers

LIFE ZONE: Subalpine, alpine
HABITAT: Along subalpine forest edges, moist open high meadows
HEIGHT: 2" - 8"
LOOK FOR: Spoon-shaped basal leaves, hairy stems. Many white ray flowers with deep yellow disk flowers forming a solitary head on stem. Phyllaries covered with dark purple/black woolly hairs.
BLOOM: Mid-summer-autumn

ROCKY MOUNTAIN ALPINE WILDFLOWERS

COULTER'S DAISY
Erigeron coulteri
Sunflower Family
(Asteraceae)

White/Cream/Green Flowers

LIFE ZONE: Subalpine, alpine
HABITAT: Subalpine open forest, high open meadows, dry and moist soils
HEIGHT: 10" - 24"
LOOK FOR: Basal leaves entire or slightly toothed, egg-shaped. Stem leaves alternate, hairy. Bright white narrow ray flowers with yellow disk flowers. Usually a solitary flower head on a hairy stem. Black and white hairs cover phyllaries.
BLOOM: Summer-autumn

White/Cream/Green Flowers

YARROW
Achillea millefolium
Sunflower Family
(Asteraceae)

LIFE ZONE: Foothills, montane, subalpine, alpine
HABITAT: Gravelly soil, open meadows, tundra slopes
HEIGHT: 6" - 24"
LOOK FOR: Leaves fern-like growing alternately on stem. White ray flowers (rarely pink) with five petals, pale yellow disk flowers forming compacted flat-topped clusters.
BLOOM: Summer-autumn

AMERICAN FALSE CANDYTUFT
Smelowskia americana
Mustard Family (Brassicaceae)

White/Cream/Green Flowers

LIFE ZONE: Alpine
HABITAT: Open, rocky alpine meadows and ridges
HEIGHT: 2" - 8"
LOOK FOR: Mostly basal leaves, fern-like, finely divided. Clusters of small flowers with four petals often white, but can be pink/lavender. Frequently grows in clumps spreading on rocky tundra slopes.
BLOOM: Summer

White/Cream/Green Flowers

LIFE ZONE: Montane, subalpine, alpine
HABITAT: Forest openings, rocky ground in the alpine.
HEIGHT: 3" - 12", lower end in the alpine
LOOK FOR: Basal leaves spoon-shaped, entire or toothed. Alternate, clasping stem leaves. Clusters of small flowers white to shades of pink with four petals forming a cross-shape, characteristic of the mustard family.
BLOOM: Early spring flower in montane, higher elevations blooms throughout the summer

**WILD CANDYTUFT
(MOUNTAIN CANDYTUFT,
ALPINE PENNYCRESS)**
Nocceae fendleri
Mustard Family (Brassicaceae)

ROCKY MOUNTAIN ALPINE WILDFLOWERS

White/Cream/Green Flowers

ALPINE SANDWORT
(ALPINE STITCHWORT)
Minuartia obtusiloba
Pink Family (Caryophyllaceae)

LIFE ZONE: Alpine
HABITAT: Dry, rocky soil, tundra slopes
HEIGHT: ¼" - 2"
LOOK FOR: Moss-like dark green basal leaves forming mats. Tiny white flowers with five rounded petals on top of minute stems covering mats.
BLOOM: Summer

FENDLER'S SANDWORT
Eremogone fendleri
Pink Family
(Caryophyllaceae)

White/Cream/Green Flowers

LIFE ZONE: Montane, subalpine, alpine
HABITAT: Rocky, sandy soil, open areas in forest and tundra slopes
HEIGHT: 4" - 12"
LOOK FOR: Thin, rigid leaves in opposite pairs along upright stalk-like stems forming dense mats. White flowers with five petals and reddish/pink anthers.
BLOOM: Summer

ROCKY MOUNTAIN ALPINE WILDFLOWERS

White/Cream/Green Flowers

LONG-STALKED STARWORT
Stellaria longipes
Pink Family
(Caryophyllaceae)

LIFE ZONE: Montane, subalpine, alpine
HABITAT: Moist forest edges, moist high meadows
HEIGHT: 4" - 8"
LOOK FOR: Smooth, narrow leaves, often upright, opposite on slender stem. One to three bright white flowers per stem. Petals deeply cut. Sepals are shorter than petals.
BLOOM: Summer

MOUSE-EAR CHICKWEED
Cerastium arvense
Pink Family
(Caryophyllaceae)

White/Cream/Green Flowers

LIFE ZONE: Foothills, montane, subalpine, alpine
HABITAT: Meadows, forest, tundra
HEIGHT: 2" - 8"
LOOK FOR: Few opposite leaves, linear to lanceolate, on branching hairy stems. White flowers with five petals, each petal divided at the tip.
BLOOM: Early spring bloom in low elevations, blooms throughout the summer in higher elevations.

ROCKY MOUNTAIN ALPINE WILDFLOWERS

White/Cream/Green Flowers

ROCKY MOUNTAIN NAILWORT
Paronychia pulvinata
Pink Family (Caryophyllaceae)

LIFE ZONE: Alpine
HABITAT: Rocky alpine meadows and ridges, fellfields, gravelly soil
HEIGHT: ½" - 2"
LOOK FOR: Woody-like stems hugging the ground or rocks. Dense mats of narrow leaves with sharp tips. Solitary, tiny greenish-yellow flowers on minute stems crowded in the leaves.
BLOOM: Summer

28   ROCKY MOUNTAIN ALPINE WILDFLOWERS

White/Cream/Green Flowers

ARCTIC GENTIAN
Gentiana algida
Gentian Family
(Gentianaceae)

LIFE ZONE: Subalpine, alpine
HABITAT: Moist alpine meadows, open tundra slopes
HEIGHT: 2" - 8"
LOOK FOR: Linear, smooth, grass-like basal leaves. Creamy white-greenish tubular shaped flowers, petals have pointed tips, purple streaks on the outside with purple-green spots on the inside of petals.
BLOOM: Late summer-autumn

ROCKY MOUNTAIN ALPINE WILDFLOWERS

ALP-LILY
Lloydia serotina
Lily Family (Liliaceae)

LIFE ZONE: Subalpine, alpine
HABITAT: Rocky ridges, slopes, high meadows
HEIGHT: 2" - 6"
LOOK FOR: Narrow, slender basal leaves, alternate stem leaves. A delicate creamy-white single flower on slender stem with six tepals, yellow at the base with pale greenish-purple veins.
BLOOM: Summer

MOUNTAIN DEATH CAMAS
(WAND LILY)
Anticlea elegans
Synonym: *Zigadenus elegans*
False Hellebore Family
(Melanthiaceae)

White/Cream/Green Flowers

LIFE ZONE: Montane, subalpine, alpine
HABITAT: Dry and moist slopes, meadows, tundra
HEIGHT: 6" - 20"
LOOK FOR: Leaves linear, long and smooth. Creamy-white star-shaped flowers, six tepals, with green glands arranged in a loose raceme. Poisonous plant.
BLOOM: Summer

ROCKY MOUNTAIN ALPINE WILDFLOWERS

White/Cream/Green Flowers

ALPINE SPRING BEAUTY
(BIG-ROOTED SPRING BEAUTY)
Claytonia megarhiza
Miner's Lettuce Family (Montiaceae)

LIFE ZONE: Alpine
HABITAT: Scree slopes, rock crevices, dry gravelly soils
HEIGHT: 2" - 6"
LOOK FOR: A rosette of thick smooth, spoon-shaped dark green/reddish basal leaves. Flowers have five white-pinkish petals with pink veins.
BLOOM: Summer

ROCKY MOUNTAIN ALPINE WILDFLOWERS

HOODED LADY'S TRESSES
Spiranthes romanzoffiana
Orchid Family (Orchidaceae)

White/Cream/Green Flowers

LIFE ZONE: Montane, subalpine
HABITAT: Moist meadows, open areas
HEIGHT: 3" - 12"
LOOK FOR: Upright basal leaves, lance-shaped, alternate on stem. Abundance of white flowers tightly spiraled on spike. Two petals, three sepals form a hood over lower lip petal.
BLOOM: Summer-autumn

White/Cream/Green Flowers

WHITE BOG ORCHID
(SCENTBOTTLE ORCHID)
Platanthera dilatata
Synonym: *Limnorchis dilatata*
Orchid Family (Orchidaceae)

LIFE ZONE: Montane, subalpine, alpine
HABITAT: Shade to sunny areas, wet areas, bogs
HEIGHT: 5" - 24"
LOOK FOR: Upright basal leaves, alternate stem leaves, smooth. A raceme of white flowers densely packed on stem. Flowers have an upper hood, two petals spreading back, lip petal tapered, back spur. Fragrant.
BLOOM: Summer

White/Cream/Green Flowers

PARRY'S LOUSEWORT
Pedicularis parryi
Broomrape Family
(Orobanchaceae)

LIFE ZONE: Subalpine, alpine
HABITAT: Dry high meadows
HEIGHT: 4" - 16"
LOOK FOR: Leaves pinnately divided, fern-like, toothed margins. Creamy white to pale yellow flowers petals curved "beaked" clustered on top of smooth stem; spike-like raceme.
BLOOM: Mid-summer-autumn

ROCKY MOUNTAIN ALPINE WILDFLOWERS

White/Cream/Green Flowers

FRINGED GRASS-OF-PARNASSUS
Parnassia fimbriata
Grass-of-Parnassus Family (Parnassiaceae)

LIFE ZONE: Subalpine, alpine
HABITAT: Wet, shaded areas, bogs, along streams
HEIGHT: 4" - 15"
LOOK FOR: Thick heart or kidney-shaped basal leaves, entire. A single white flower on a stem with five petals fringed on the lower half of petals, five green sepals, and protruding green pistil.
BLOOM: Mid-summer-autumn

White/Cream/Green Flowers

SNOWLOVER
(ROCKY MOUNTAIN SNOWLOVER)
Chionophila jamesii
Plantain Family (Plantaginaceae)

LIFE ZONE: Alpine
HABITAT: Open tundra slopes
HEIGHT: 2" - 4"
LOOK FOR: Mainly basal leaves, thick, linear pointing upward. Creamy white tubular flowers with tinge of purple clustered, usually on one side of stem.
BLOOM: Summer

White/Cream/Green Flowers

ALPINE PHLOX
Phlox condensate
Phlox Family
(Polemoniaceae)

LIFE ZONE: Alpine
HABITAT: Open, rocky tundra slopes
HEIGHT: Less than 1"
LOOK FOR: Thick cushion plant. Tiny oblong-linear leaves, slightly hairy or smooth with sharp tips forming thick mats. Small flowers with five petals white, pink or pale blue crowding mat surface. Fragrant.
BLOOM: Summer

White/Cream/Green Flowers

BRANDEGEE'S SKY PILOT
(HONEY SKY PILOT OR POLEMONIUM)
Polemonium brandegeei
Phlox Family (Polemoniaceae)

LIFE ZONE: Subalpine, alpine
HABITAT: Around boulders, rock outcroppings, cliffs, crevices
HEIGHT: 4" - 12"
LOOK FOR: Leaves ladder-like, pinnately compound, many leaflets. Clusters of white-creamy tubular flowers with stamens topped with bright yellow anthers.
BLOOM: Summer

GLOBE GILIA
(HOOSIER PASS IPOMOPSIS)
Ipomopsis globularis
Phlox Family (Polemoniaceae)

White/Cream/Green Flowers

LIFE ZONE: Alpine
HABITAT: High meadows, tundra slopes, ridges
HEIGHT: 2" - 6"
LOOK FOR: Slender linear leaves divided into several narrow segments, woolly cobwebby hairs. Ball-like clusters of white-pale lavender flowers surrounded by silky hairs. Fragrant. Uncommon alpine plant, with limited ranges, endemic.
BLOOM: Mid-summer

ALPINE BISTORT
Bistorta vivipara
Buckwheat Family
(Polygonaceae)

White/Cream/Green Flowers

LIFE ZONE: Subalpine, alpine
HABITAT: Moist areas, grassy open meadows, tundra
HEIGHT: 4" - 12"
LOOK FOR: Narrow linear basal leaves, few alternate stem leaves. Slender stem holds white-pinkish flowers in elongated clusters. Dark reddish/brown bulblets below flower clusters that fall to the ground growing new plants.
BLOOM: Summer

ROCKY MOUNTAIN ALPINE WILDFLOWERS

White/Cream/Green Flowers

ALPINE MOUNTAIN SORREL
Oxyria digyna
Buckwheat Family (Polygonaceae)

LIFE ZONE: Subalpine, alpine
HABITAT: Rocky ground, nestled in boulders, alpine meadows
HEIGHT: 4" - 24"
LOOK FOR: Kidney-shaped rounded basal leaves, entire, may have reddish tints. Tiny greenish-reddish flowers in dense clusters on erect hairless spike-like stem.
BLOOM: Summer-autumn

White/Cream/Green Flowers

AMERICAN BISTORT
Bistorta bistortoides
Buckwheat Family
(Polygonaceae)

LIFE ZONE: Montane, subalpine, alpine
HABITAT: Moist meadows, open high meadows, tundra slopes
HEIGHT: 7" - 24"
LOOK FOR: Basal and alternate narrow leaves. White-pinkish flowers with protruding stamens in a compact cylinder shape on a slender stalk.
BLOOM: Summer

SUBALPINE SULFUR FLOWER
Eriogonum umbellatum var. majus
Buckwheat Family (Polygonaceae)

White/Cream/Green Flowers

LIFE ZONE: Subalpine, alpine
HABITAT: Open meadows, rocky ground
HEIGHT: 8" - 16"
LOOK FOR: Basal leaves oval, forming mats. Leafless stems covered with fine white hairs. Creamy-white flowers clustered on umbels. Flowers turn pinkish/orange with age. Often grows in patches.
BLOOM: Mid-summer-autumn

ROCKY MOUNTAIN ALPINE WILDFLOWERS

PYGMY-FLOWER ROCK JASMINE
(NORTHERN FAIRY CANDELABRA)
Androsace septentrionalis
Primrose Family (Primulaceae)

White/Cream/Green Flowers

LIFE ZONE: Foothills, montane, subalpine, alpine
HABITAT: Forest, open meadows, tundra slopes
HEIGHT: 2" - 6"
LOOK FOR: Tiny rosette basal leaves. Flowers with five tiny white petals, yellow centers on upright minute stems.
BLOOM: Summer

White/Cream/Green Flowers

ROCK JASMINE
(SWEET-FLOWER ROCK JASMINE)
Androsace chamaejasme
Primrose Family (Primulaceae)

LIFE ZONE: Alpine
HABITAT: Tundra, rocky slopes
HEIGHT: 1" - 3"
LOOK FOR: Mat forming basal rosette leaves, hairy margins. Clusters of delicate white-creamy flowers on minute stems with yellow centers turning pinkish as ages.
BLOOM: Summer

White/Cream/Green Flowers

GLOBEFLOWER
Trollius albiflorus
Buttercup Family
(Ranunculaceae)

LIFE ZONE: Subalpine, alpine
HABITAT: Subalpine forest, streamsides, moist alpine meadows
HEIGHT: 4" - 20"
LOOK FOR: Basal and alternate leaves palmately divided, toothed, hairless stems. Creamy-white flowers consist of five-nine petal-like sepals and bright yellow stamens in center. Tiny yellow petals surround the base of the stamens.
BLOOM: Late spring-summer

White/Cream/Green Flowers

MARSH MARIGOLD
Caltha leptosepala
Buttercup Family
(Ranunculaceae)

LIFE ZONE: Subalpine, alpine
HABITAT: Moist meadows, along streams
HEIGHT: 2" - 8"
LOOK FOR: Large, smooth oblong leaves, wavy margins. White flowers with bluish streaks underneath the petal-like sepals on a leafless stem. Abundant golden stamens in the center. Often grows in batches among globeflowers.
BLOOM: Summer

White/Cream/Green Flowers

NARCISSUS ANEMONE
Amemone narcissiflora
Buttercup Family
(Ranunculaceae)

LIFE ZONE: Sub-alpine, alpine
HABITAT: Moist high meadows, slopes
HEIGHT: 4" - 18".
LOOK FOR: Mainly basal leaves, palmately divided, deeply lobed and hairy. Leaves on stems whorled and/or opposite. Stems are covered with long wispy hairs. Creamy white petal-like sepals with numerous golden stamens in the center.
BLOOM: Summer

White/Cream/Green Flowers

MOUNTAIN DRYAD
(MOUNTAIN AVENS)
Dryas octopetala
Rose Family (Rosaceae)

LIFE ZONE: Alpine
HABITAT: High meadows, ridges, gravelly, rocky soil
HEIGHT: The leafless flower stem 4" - 8"
LOOK FOR: Dark green leathery, oblong shaped leaves, rounded toothed margins, hairy underneath and mat forming. Creamy white flowers, usually eight petals, with numerous yellow stamens in the center.
BLOOM: Summer

ALPINE WILLOW
(ROCK WILLOW)
Salix petrophila
Willow Family (Salicaceae)

White/Cream/Green Flowers

LIFE ZONE: Alpine
HABITAT: Open tundra slopes, high meadows often grows among Snow Willow
HEIGHT: 2" - 8"
LOOK FOR: Broad, bright green leaves, pointed or slightly rounded tips, hairs maybe present or absent. Reddish-brown woody stems along the ground. Flowers (catkins) elongated on short spikes. A dioecious plant. Fruits open to fluffy seeds.
BLOOM: Mid-summer-autumn

ROCKY MOUNTAIN ALPINE WILDFLOWERS

White/Cream/Green Flowers

SNOW WILLOW
Salix nivalis
Synonym: *Salix reticulata*
Willow Family (Salicaceae)

LIFE ZONE: Alpine
HABITAT: Open tundra slopes, high meadows
HEIGHT: ½" - 2"
LOOK FOR: Rounded leaves with a prominent netted vein pattern, slightly hairy to smooth. Tiny flowers (catkins) in among the leaves. A dioecious plant.
BLOOM: Summer

DOTTED SAXIFRAGE

Saxifraga austromontana
Synonyms: *Cilaria austromontana*
Saxifrage Family (Saxifragaceae)

White/Cream/Green Flowers

LIFE ZONE: Foothills, montane, subalpine, alpine
HABITAT: Spruce-fir forest, rocky soil, rock outcroppings, tundra
HEIGHT: 2" - 6"
LOOK FOR: Dark green basal leaves forming mats. Tiny alternate leaves on stem. Small white flowers with five petals dotted red, yellow and/or orange.
BLOOM: Summer

ROCKY MOUNTAIN ALPINE WILDFLOWERS

White/Cream/Green Flowers

FRONT RANGE ALUMROOT
(Hall's Alumroot)
Heuchera hallii
Saxifrage Family
(Saxifragaceae)

LIFE ZONE: Montane, subalpine, alpine
HABITAT: Rock crevices, cliffsides
HEIGHT: 4" - 12"
LOOK FOR: Rounded kidney-shaped basal leaves deeply lobed margins. Compact clusters of white-cream bell-shaped flowers on erect leafless stems. Endemic to the Front Range of Colorado.
BLOOM: Summer

NODDING SAXIFRAGE
Saxifraga cernua
Saxifrage Family (Saxifragaceae)

White/Cream/Green Flowers

LIFE ZONE: Alpine
HABITAT: Rocky areas, fellfields, along shady rock outcroppings and cliffs
HEIGHT: 4" - 6"
LOOK FOR: Mostly basal leaves rounded and deeply lobed. Reddish bulblets below the flower along stem and in leaf axils. Solitary white flower often "nodding" on a hairy stem.
BLOOM: Mid-summer

White/Cream/Green Flowers

ROCKY MOUNTAIN ALUMROOT
(Bracted Alumroot)
Heuchera bracteata
Saxifrage Family
(Saxifragaceae)

LIFE ZONE: Montane, subalpine, alpine
HABITAT: Dry areas, rocky ledges, rock crevices
HEIGHT: 6" - 12"
LOOK FOR: Lobed basal leaves with sharply toothed margins. Dense clusters of tiny white-greenish narrow bell-shaped flowers on spike-like hairy stalk.
BLOOM: Summer

SIDE-FLOWERED MITREWORT
(White Mitrewort)
Mitella stauropetala
Saxifrage Family (Saxifragaceae)

White/Cream/Green Flowers

LIFE ZONE: Montane, subalpine, alpine
HABITAT: Forest edges, moist meadows, near streams
HEIGHT: 12" - 16"
LOOK FOR: Large, basal leaves rounded with rounded teeth on margins. Tiny cupped-shaped white flowers, three lobed narrow petals flaring out, rounded sepals. Flowers arranged on one side of a slender stem.
BLOOM: Early-mid-summer

ROCKY MOUNTAIN ALPINE WILDFLOWERS

SNOWBALL SAXIFRAGE
(Diamond-Leaf Saxifrage)
Micranthes rhomboidea
Saxifrage Family (Saxifragaceae)

LIFE ZONE: Foothills, montane, subalpine, alpine
HABITAT: Meadows, rocky areas, tundra slopes
HEIGHT: 2" - 12"
LOOK FOR: A basal rosette of thick diamond shaped leaves with toothed margins. A slender leafless stem holding a tight round cluster of tiny white flowers with five petals.
BLOOM: Early summer-summer

White/Cream/Green Flowers

WEAK SAXIFRAGE
(Pygmy Saxifrage)
Saxifraga rivularis
Saxifrage Family
(Saxifragaceae)

White/Cream/Green Flowers

LIFE ZONE: Subalpine, alpine
HABITAT: Moist, shady rocky areas, edges of rivulets, crevices, rock ledges
HEIGHT: 3" - 8"
LOOK FOR: Basal leaves, scalloped edges, few stem leaves. Dainty plant with one-five small white flowers on a straight slender stem. Often grows in small patches.
BLOOM: Mid-summer

ROCKY MOUNTAIN ALPINE WILDFLOWERS

White/Cream/Green Flowers

SHARPLEAF VALERIAN
Valeriana acutiloba
Valerian Family (Valerianaceae)

LIFE ZONE: Montane, subalpine, alpine
HABITAT: Moist areas, forest openings, high meadows
HEIGHT: 6" - 18"
LOOK FOR: Oblong basal leaves are entire, pointed tips, few opposite leaves on erect stems. Circular, flat-topped flower clusters first appears pink turning white as opens to full bloom. Stamens protrude out beyond petals.
BLOOM: Summer

Yellow • Orange Flowers

Avalanche lily.

Yellow/Orange Flowers

ALPINE PARSLEY
Cymopterus alpinus
Synonym: *Oreoxis alpine*
Parsley Family (Apiaceae)

LIFE ZONE: Subalpine, alpine
HABITAT: High subalpine and alpine meadows, rocky tundra slopes
HEIGHT: ½" - 4"
LOOK FOR: Dwarf plant, growing low to ground. Linear basal leaves pinnately divided into leaflets spreading out. Leafless flower stems supporting clusters of tiny yellow flowers forming a flat top on umbels.
BLOOM: Summer

ALPINE SAGEWORT
(DWARF SAGEWORT)
Artemisia scopulorum
Sunflower Family (Asteraceae)

Yellow/Orange Flowers

LIFE ZONE: Subalpine, alpine
HABITAT: Rocky high meadows, tundra
HEIGHT: 3" - 12"
LOOK FOR: Basal leaves sage green-grayish and finely cut into segments. Five to twenty compact flowers composed of yellow-brownish disk flowers arranged on slender, hairy spike-like stem. Flowers erect or nodding. Phyllaries have green-black hairs with dark lined margins.
BLOOM: Mid-summer-autumn

Yellow/Orange Flowers

ARROWLEAF RAGWORT
Senecio triangularis
Sunflower Family (Asteraceae)

LIFE ZONE: Montane, subalpine, alpine
HABITAT: Moist, open areas, along streams, high meadows
HEIGHT: 1' - 5'
LOOK FOR: Alternate, arrow-shaped serrated leaves. Yellow ray flowers and disk flowers forming clusters on branching stems. Often grows in large masses.
BLOOM: Summer

BLACK-TIP RAGWORT
Senecio atratus
Sunflower Family (Asteraceae)

Yellow/Orange Flowers

LIFE ZONE: Subalpine, alpine
HABITAT: Open slopes, rocky soil
HEIGHT: 12" - 30"
LOOK FOR: Upright gray-green lance-shaped-oblong, hairy basal leaves. Hairy, slightly toothed alternate stem leaves on a rough hairy stem. Yellow ray flowers and disk flowers form flat-topped clusters. Phyllaries have black tips.
BLOOM: Mid-summer-autumn

ROCKY MOUNTAIN ALPINE WILDFLOWERS

BROADLEAF ARNICA
Arnica latifolia
Sunflower Family (Asteraceae)

Yellow/Orange Flowers

LIFE ZONE: Subalpine, alpine
HABITAT: Open high meadows
HEIGHT: 4" - 24"
LOOK FOR: Alternate leaves broad in the middle tapered at the ends, upper stem leaves sessile. Bright yellow ray and disk flowers. Green, hairy, pointed phyllaries that are equal in length.
BLOOM: Summer

COLORADO RAGWORT
Senecio soldanella
Synonym: *Ligularia soldanella*
Sunflower Family (Asteraceae)

Yellow/Orange Flowers

LIFE ZONE: Alpine
HABITAT: Scree slopes, high ridges, rocky areas
HEIGHT: 2" - 8"
LOOK FOR: Thick, smooth, rounded purple basal leaves, toothed. Solitary yellow ray flowers with numerous yellow disk flowers on short stems.
BLOOM: Mid-summer

ROCKY MOUNTAIN ALPINE WILDFLOWERS

DWARF MOUNTAIN RAGWORT
(FREMONT'S RAGWORT)
Senecio fremontii var. blitoides
Sunflower Family (Asteraceae)

Yellow/Orange Flowers

LIFE ZONE: Subalpine, alpine
HABITAT: Rocky scree slopes, talus slopes, rock outcroppings, rocky crevices
HEIGHT: 2" - 12" Spreading out several feet.
LOOK FOR: Thick, glossy green spoon-shape leaves with sharply toothed margins, sessile, alternate on stem. Yellow ray and disk flowers on a compact plant.
BLOOM: Summer

HOARY GROUNDSEL
(WERNER'S GROUNDSEL, ROCK GROUNDSEL)
Packera werneriifolia
Sunflower Family (Asteraceae)

Yellow/Orange Flowers

LIFE ZONE: Subalpine, alpine
HABITAT: gravelly soils, rocky areas, talus slopes
HEIGHT: 4" - 8"
LOOK FOR: Dark green, hairy, spoon-shaped basal leaves, entire or wavy, maybe toothed at tips forming dense mats. Five to thirteen bright yellow ray flowers with darker yellow disk flowers covering a dense mat.
BLOOM: Summer

HOLM'S RAGWORT
Senecio amplectens var. holmii
Sunflower Family (Asteraceae)

Yellow/Orange Flowers

LIFE ZONE: Subalpine, alpine
HABITAT: Scree slopes, rocky, gravelly soil
HEIGHT: 2" - 8"
LOOK FOR: Thick green/reddish/purple upright basal leaves/leaf edges purple and toothed, occasionally a few stem leaves. Phyllaries purplish. Drooping yellow ray and disk flowers.
BLOOM: Mid-summer

70 ROCKY MOUNTAIN ALPINE WILDFLOWERS

MT. ALBERT GOLDENROD
(DWARF GOLDENROD)
Solidago simplex
Sunflower Family (Asteraceae)

Yellow/Orange Flowers

LIFE ZONE: Subalpine, alpine
HABITAT: Open high meadows, tundra
HEIGHT: 2" - 12"
LOOK FOR: Basal leaves spoon-shaped or linear, few stem leaves, toothed, hairs on margins. Small rounded clusters of golden yellow flowers, five-sixteen ray flowers with tiny yellow disk flowers.
BLOOM: Summer

ROCKY MOUNTAIN ALPINE WILDFLOWERS

NODDING RAGWORT
Senecio bigelovii (Ligularia bigelovii)
Sunflower Family (Asteraceae)

Yellow/Orange Flowers

LIFE ZONE: Montane, subalpine
HABITAT: Dry open areas, hillsides, meadows
HEIGHT: 1'-3'
LOOK FOR: Lance-shaped alternate leaves. Ray flowers absent. Numerous yellow disk flowers nodding on stem. Phyllaries green turning purplish as ages. Often mistaken as an up-open flower. Lifting the flower head reveals the numerous yellow disk flowers.
BLOOM: Summer to autumn

Yellow/Orange Flowers

**OLD MAN OF THE MOUNTAIN
(ALPINE SUNFLOWER)**
Hymenoxys grandiflora
Sunflower Family (Asteraceae)

LIFE ZONE: Alpine
HABITAT: Dry, open alpine tundra slopes
HEIGHT: 2" - 10"
LOOK FOR: Basal leaves with few alternate leaves. Leaves stringy in finely lobed segments. Thick, white, wooly hairs cover stems, leaves and phyllaries. Large bright yellow ray flowers with three notches at the tips and yellow disk flowers in center. A monocarpic plant.
BLOOM: Summer

ROCKY MOUNTAIN ALPINE WILDFLOWERS

ORANGE AGOSERIS
(ORANGE MOUNTAIN DANDELION)
Agoseris aurantiaca
Sunflower Family (Asteraceae)

Yellow/Orange Flowers

LIFE ZONE: Foothills, montane, subalpine, alpine
HABITAT: Open meadows, forest edges
HEIGHT: 3" - 24" Lower end in the alpine
LOOK FOR: Narrow, linear basal leaves smooth or slightly lobed. A leafless hairy stem bearing a single burnt-orange ray flower, rarely pink. Disk flowers absent. Tiny teeth on tips of petals.
BLOOM: Summer

PALE AGOSERIS
(MOUNTAIN DANDELION)
Agoseris glauca
Sunflower Family (Asteraceae)

Yellow/Orange Flowers

LIFE ZONE: Montane, subalpine, alpine
HABITAT: Open meadows, rocky areas
HEIGHT: 8" - 24" Shorter end in alpine
LOOK FOR: Long, upright basal leaves, maybe hairy or smooth. Hairy, green phyllaries green-purplish streaks. Bright yellow ray flowers, disk flowers absent. A solitary flower on a leafless stem.
BLOOM: Summer

ROCKY MOUNTAIN ALPINE WILDFLOWERS

PARRY'S ARNICA
(RAYLESS ARNICA)
Arnica parryi
Sunflower Family (Asteraceae)

Yellow/Orange Flowers

LIFE ZONE: Subalpine, alpine
HABITAT: Open forest and high meadows
HEIGHT: 10" - 20"
LOOK FOR: Lance-shaped hairy basal leaves, opposite leaves on hairy stem. Ray flowers absent. Numerous compact yellow disk flowers, erect or nodding.
BLOOM: Summer

PYGMY GOLDENWEED
(SMALL SUNSPOT)
Tonestus pygmaeus
Sunflower Family (Asteraceae)

Yellow/Orange Flowers

LIFE ZONE: Alpine
HABITAT: Open, rocky, dry areas, tundra
HEIGHT: 1" - 4"
LOOK FOR: Narrow basal leaves entire with fine hairs on margins, forms small clumps. Solitary bright yellow ray and disk flowers on a leafless stem. No notches on petal tips. Phyllaries have fine hairs on margins.
BLOOM: Summer

ROCKY MOUNTAIN ALPINE WILDFLOWERS

SAFFRON RAGWORT
Packera crocata
Sunflower Family (Asteraceae)

Yellow/Orange Flowers

LIFE ZONE: Subalpine, alpine
HABITAT: Grassy openings, moist high meadows
HEIGHT: 4" - 30"
LOOK FOR: Basal leaves ovate and upright, smaller stem leaves maybe lobed or slightly toothed. Bright yellow-orange ray flowers with darker yellow disks flowers.
BLOOM: Mid-summer

SHOWY ALPINE RAGWORT
Senecio amplectens var. *amplectens*
Sunflower Family (Asteraceae)

Yellow/Orange Flowers

LIFE ZONE: Subalpine, alpine
HABITAT: Subalpine forest edges, alpine meadows
HEIGHT: 12" - 24"
LOOK FOR: Long basal leaves, shorter stem leaves, toothed. Lemon-yellow ray flowers, petal tips pointed, darker disk flowers. Phyllaries have dark edges. Flowers tend to nod on erect stems. Usually grows in patches.
BLOOM: Mid-summer

ROCKY MOUNTAIN ALPINE WILDFLOWERS

STEMLESS FOUR-NERVE DAISY
(GOLDFLOWER)
Tetraneuris acaulis var. *caespitosa*
Synonym: *Hymenoyxs acaulis*
Sunflower Family (Asteraceae)

Yellow/Orange Flowers

LIFE ZONE: Alpine
HABITAT: Rocky areas, tundra slopes
HEIGHT: 1" - 3"
LOOK FOR: Woolly, hairy basal leaves, entire, spoon shaped or lanceolate. Small yellow ray and disk flowers with three notches at tips of petals. Solitary head on a leafless stem. Woolly-hairy phyllaries.
BLOOM: Summer

ALPINE TWINPOD
Physaria alpina
Mustard Family (Brassicaceae)

Yellow/Orange Flowers

LIFE ZONE: Alpine
HABITAT: Rocky tundra and ridges
HEIGHT: 2" - 6" spreading out
LOOK FOR: Gray-green rosette of basal leaves spoon shaped – or widest at the top, smooth or slightly toothed, fine hairs, stems spreading along the ground. Bright yellow flowers with four petals, upright. Endemic.
BLOOM: Summer

ROCKY MOUNTAIN ALPINE WILDFLOWERS

ALPINE WALLFLOWER
(WESTERN WALLFLOWER)
Erysimum capitatum
Mustard Family (Brassicaceae)

LIFE ZONE: Foothills, montane, subalpine, alpine
HABITAT: Rocky ground, tundra slopes in alpine
HEIGHT: 2" - 6" in alpine, up to 36" in lower elevations
LOOK FOR: Narrow leaves, alternate on stem, mostly basal in the alpine. Rounded cluster of bright yellow flowers, four petals, can vary colors yellow, orange, or lavender.
BLOOM: Summer

Yellow/Orange Flowers

GOLDEN DRABA
Draba aurea
Mustard Family (Brassicaceae)

LIFE ZONE: Montane, subalpine, alpine
HABITAT: Rocky soil, forest edges, tundra
HEIGHT: 2" - 20" Shorter end in alpine
LOOK FOR: Basal leaves oblong forms rosette, few upright leaves clasping the stem, slightly toothed, hairy. Yellow flowers with four petals forming a cross shape, characteristic of the pea family. Flowers form clusters on top of stems.
BLOOM: Summer

Yellow/Orange Flowers

THICK DRABA
Draba crassa
Mustard Family (Brassicaceae)

LIFE ZONE: Alpine
HABITAT: Rocky alpine ridges, talus slopes
HEIGHT: 3" - 8"
LOOK FOR: Thick, slightly hairy to glabrous basal leaves forming a rosette. Bright yellow four petals flower on short stems.
BLOOM: Summer

YELLOW STONECROP
Sedum lanceolatum
Stonecrop Family (Crassulaceae)

Yellow/Orange Flowers

LIFE ZONE: Foothills, montane, subalpine, alpine
HABITAT: Sunny, dry, rocky soil
HEIGHT: 2" - 6"
LOOK FOR: Succulent-like basal leaves and alternate lance-shaped leaves on short stems. Gold star-shape flowers with five petals forming clusters.
BLOOM: Summer

Yellow/Orange Flowers

AVALANCHE LILY
(GLACIER LILY)
Erythronium grandiflorum
Lily Family (Liliaceae)

LIFE ZONE: Montane, subalpine, alpine
HABITAT: Moist areas, along melting snowbeds
HEIGHT: 4" - 15"
LOOK FOR: Two bright green, long pointed basal leaves. Bright yellow flowers with curving back petals that often droop, six golden/reddish stamens. Usually a single flower per stem.
BLOOM: Early summer-mid-summer

ALPINE PAINTBRUSH
(SHORTFLOWER INDIAN PAINTBRUSH)
Castilleja puberula
Broomrape Family (Orobanchaceae)

Yellow/Orange Flowers

LIFE ZONE: Alpine
HABITAT: Alpine slopes, ridges, tundra
HEIGHT: 3" - 6"
LOOK FOR: Leaves linear, entire with fine hairs. Flowers pale-yellow with fine hairs.
BLOOM: Summer

ROCKY MOUNTAIN ALPINE WILDFLOWERS

FERN LEAF LOUSEWORT
(BRACTED OR PAYSON'S LOUSEWORT)
Pedicularis bracteosa
Broomrape Family (Orobanchaceae)

Yellow/Orange Flowers

LIFE ZONE: Montane, subalpine, alpine
HABITAT: Forest, dry meadows, and rocky slopes
HEIGHT: 1' - 3'
LOOK FOR: Leaves pinnately divided, fern-like, alternate. Yellowish beaked flowers in clusters on spike-like hairy stem.
BLOOM: Summer

WESTERN YELLOW PAINTBRUSH
Castilleja occidentalis
Broomrape Family
(Orobanchaceae)

Yellow/Orange Flowers

LIFE ZONE: Subalpine, alpine
HABITAT: Rocky, open tundra and meadows
HEIGHT: 5" - 8"
LOOK FOR: Alternate, lance-shaped hairy leaves. Flowers pale-yellow bracts and sepals. Often hybridizes resulting in mixed white/red/pinks/purples.
BLOOM: Summer

ALPINE POPPY
(ARCTIC POPPY, KLUANE POPPY)
Papaver radicatum ssp. kluanensis
Poppy Family (Papaveraceae)

Yellow/Orange Flowers

LIFE ZONE: Alpine
HABITAT: Dry alpine tundra, rocky alpine meadows, scree slopes
HEIGHT: 3" - 6"
LOOK FOR: Gray-green basal leaves, pinnately dissected, deeply lobed with fine hairs. Leafless stems hold solitary lemon yellow flower with numerous stamens. A rare alpine flower.
BLOOM: Summer

SUBALPINE MONKEYFLOWER
Mimulus tilingii
Lopseed Family (Phrymaceae)

Yellow/Orange Flowers

LIFE ZONE: Subalpine, alpine
HABITAT: Along streams, seeps
HEIGHT: 1" - 8"
LOOK FOR: Low growing plant often spreading out on the ground in mats. Oval-rounded leaves deeply veined, opposite, slightly toothed on margins, slightly hairy. Tubular yellow flower, lobed, with pale to deep red spots and hairs on inside of lobes. Usually one to three flowers per stem.
BLOOM: Mid-summer-autumn

ALPINE GOLDEN BUCKWHEAT
Eriogonum flavum
Buckwheat Family (Polygonaceae)

Yellow/Orange Flowers

LIFE ZONE: Foothills, montane, subalpine, alpine
HABITAT: Scree slopes, gravelly soils, open tundra slopes
HEIGHT: 2" - 3" in the alpine, taller in lower elevations
LOOK FOR: Dark to grayish-green basal leaves, oblong and broad in middle with fine hairs forming compact mats. Tight clusters of tiny golden yellow flowers on hairy short stems.
BLOOM: Mid-summer

ESCHSCHOLTZ'S BUTTERCUP
(SUBALPINE BUTTERCUP)
Ranunculus eschscholtzii
Buttercup Family (Ranunculaceae)

Yellow/Orange Flowers

LIFE ZONE: Subalpine, alpine
HABITAT: Moist areas, along streams, edges of melting snowbeds, subalpine forest
HEIGHT: 2" - 10"
LOOK FOR: Deeply cut leaves divided to 3 lobes. Glossy, bright yellow flowers with five over-lapping petals.
BLOOM: Summer

ROCKY MOUNTAIN ALPINE WILDFLOWERS

ROCKY MOUNTAIN BUTTERCUP
(MACAULEY'S BUTTERCUP)
Ranunculus macauleyi
Buttercup Family (Ranunculaceae)

Yellow/Orange Flowers

LIFE ZONE: Subalpine, alpine
HABITAT: Open, moist high meadows, edges of melting snowbeds, tundra
HEIGHT: 2" - 6"
LOOK FOR: Bright green lanceolate leaves notched at the tip. Bright, shiny yellow flowers, five petals. Bracts covered with fuzzy thick black/brown hairs.
BLOOM: Summer

Yellow/Orange Flowers

SNOW BUTTERCUP
(ALPINE BUTTERCUP)
Ranunculus adoneus
Buttercup Family (Ranunculaceae)

LIFE ZONE: Subalpine, alpine
HABITAT: Along melting snowbeds, open moist areas, tundra
HEIGHT: 4" - 8"
LOOK FOR: String-like leaves divided into segments with five glossy yellow petals growing in small clusters.
BLOOM: Early summer-summer

ROCKY MOUNTAIN ALPINE WILDFLOWERS

Yellow/Orange Flowers

ALPINE AVENS
Geum rossii
Rose Family (Rosaceae)

LIFE ZONE: Alpine
HABITAT: Sunny rocky slopes and tundra
HEIGHT: 2" - 10"
LOOK FOR: Bright green leaves pinnately divided, fern-like. Five rounded sunny yellow petals forming cup-shaped flowers. Often covers large areas on the tundra. Leaves turn brilliant red in autumn. A favorite food source for the pika.
BLOOM: Summer

ALPINE IVESIA
Ivesia gordonii
Rose Family (Rosaceae)

Yellow/Orange Flowers

LIFE ZONE: Montane, subalpine, alpine
HABITAT: Dry, rocky slopes
HEIGHT: 6" - 12"
LOOK FOR: Woody base, upright fern-like leaves. Bright yellow clusters of five spoon-shaped pointed petals on hairy leafless stems. Flowers turn orange-red as ages.
BLOOM: Late spring-autumn

ROCKY MOUNTAIN ALPINE WILDFLOWERS

SIBBALDIA
(CREEPING SIBBALDIA, CLOVERLEAF ROSE)
Sibbaldia procumbens
Rose Family (Rosaceae)

Yellow/Orange Flowers

LIFE ZONE: Montane, subalpine, alpine
HABITAT: Open meadows, forest edges, tundra slopes, melting snowbeds at high elevations
HEIGHT: 2" - 4"
LOOK FOR: Veined Leaves, slightly hairy and divided into three leaflets, toothed at tip, mat forming and spreading. Tiny flowers with five pale yellow-greenish petals and five longer green sepals.
BLOOM: Summer

Yellow/Orange Flowers

GOLDEN SAXIFRAGE
(GOLDBLOOM SAXIFRAGE)

Saxifraga chrysantha
Saxifrage Family (Saxifragaceae)

LIFE ZONE: Alpine
HABITAT: Alpine meadows, rocky ground, scree slopes
HEIGHT: 2" - 4"
LOOK FOR: Tiny basal leaves in rosettes forming mats, few stem leaves. Dainty golden yellow flowers, five petals with orange-dark yellow spots.
BLOOM: Summer

ROCKY MOUNTAIN ALPINE WILDFLOWERS

Yellow/Orange Flowers

LIFE ZONE: Montane, subalpine, alpine
HABITAT: Rocky outcroppings, rock crevices
HEIGHT: 8" - 12" (taller version grows in lower elevations)
LOOK FOR: Leaves kidney-shaped/rounded, deeply lobed, toothed margins. Tiny yellow-white cup-shaped flower clusters elongated on tall leafless hairy stems.
BLOOM: Summer

LITTLE-LEAF ALUMROOT
(COMMON ALUMROOT)
Heuhera parvifolia
Saxifrage Family
(Saxifragaceae)

ROCKY MOUNTAIN ALPINE WILDFLOWERS

WHIPLASH SAXIFRAGE
Saxifraga flagellaris
Saxifrage Family
(Saxifragaceae)

Yellow/Orange Flowers

LIFE ZONE: Alpine
HABITAT: Rocky ground, open alpine meadows and scree slopes
HEIGHT: 2" - 6"
LOOK FOR: Basal rosette of leaves, long red runners on the ground, stem leaves alternate. Stems and leaves covered with reddish glandular hairs, leaves sharply tipped. Dainty, bright gold flowers with five petals.
BLOOM: Summer

ROCKY MOUNTAIN ALPINE WILDFLOWERS

Yellow/Orange Flowers

ARCTIC YELLOW VIOLET
Viola biflora
Violet Family (Violaceae)

LIFE ZONE: Subalpine, alpine
HABITAT: Moist areas, under shelter of boulders, rock outcroppings, scree slopes
HEIGHT: 1" - 3"
LOOK FOR: Bright green kidney-shaped leaves, small teeth and hairs on leaf margins. Yellow flower petals streaked with brown/purplish lines. Head of style divided into two parts. Uncommon alpine plant.
BLOOM: Early-mid-summer

Red • Pink Flowers

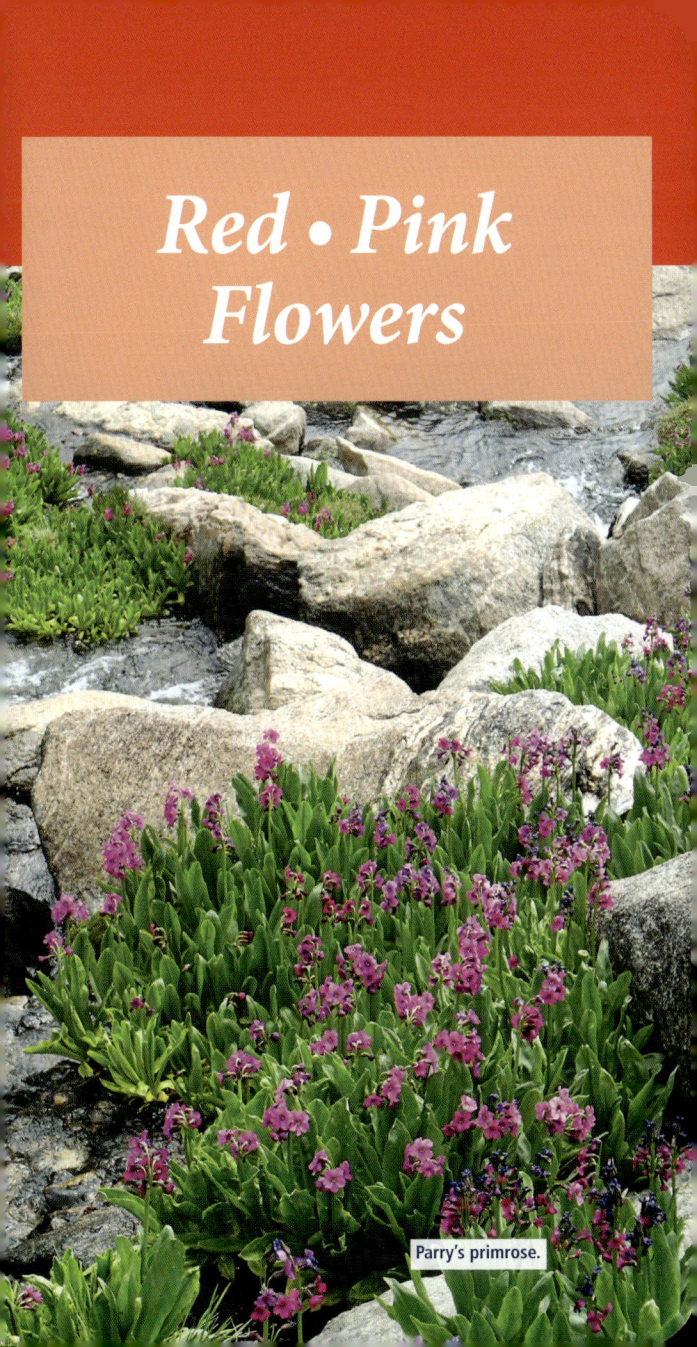

Parry's primrose.

GLACIER DAISY
(SUBALPINE DAISY)
Erigeron glacialis
Synonym: *Erigeron peregrinus*
Sunflower Family (Asteraceae)

LIFE ZONE: Subalpine
HABITAT: Moist meadows, tundra
HEIGHT: 4" - 18"
LOOK FOR: Narrow basal leaves, stem leaves lanceolate, hairless or slightly hairy. Wide ray flowers vary in color from pink, lavender, purple or white with yellow disks flowers. White hairs on stem below phyllaries. Phyllaries have red pointed tips and fine red glandular hairs.
BLOOM: Summer

TALL DAISY
(TALL FLEABANE, BEAUTIFUL DAISY)
Erigeron elatior
Sunflower Family (Asteraceae)

Red/Pink Flowers

LIFE ZONE: Montane, subalpine
HABITAT: Forest edges, meadows, moist areas
HEIGHT: 8" - 24"
LOOK FOR: Alternate, lanceolate, sparsely hairy leaves, entire, pointed tip. A certain characteristic is the pink-whitish wooly hairs under the flower head. Light pink-lavender narrow ray flowers, yellow disks flowers on a hairy stem. Often grows in eye-catching bunches.
BLOOM: Mid-summer

ROCKY MOUNTAIN ALPINE WILDFLOWERS

MOSS CAMPION
Silene acaulis
Pink Family
(Caryophyllaceae)

Red/Pink Flowers

LIFE ZONE: Alpine
HABITAT: Rocky soil, rock outcroppings, tundra slopes
HEIGHT: 1" - 2"
LOOK FOR: Evergreen leaves with pointed tips forming mats. Tiny deep pink-lavender flowers with five petals notched at the tips on minute stems.
BLOOM: Summer

Red/Pink Flowers

LIFE ZONE: Subalpine, alpine
HABITAT: Moist and dry areas, high meadows, rocky slopes
HEIGHT: 4" - 12"
LOOK FOR: Succulent flat leaves with pointed tips alternate on stem. Maroon-deep-red flowers forming flat-topped clusters on upright stems.
BLOOM: Summer

KING'S CROWN
Rhodiola integrifolia
Stonecrop Family
(Crassulaceae)

ROCKY MOUNTAIN ALPINE WILDFLOWERS

QUEEN'S CROWN
(ROSE CROWN)
Rhodiola rhodantha
Stonecrop Family (Crassulaceae)

Red/Pink Flowers

LIFE ZONE: Subalpine, alpine
HABITAT: Wet areas, marshes, near streams
HEIGHT: 4" - 12"
LOOK FOR: Succulent flat leaves with pointed tips alternate on stem. Flower clusters of deep rosy color or light pink forming a rounded cylinder-like flower head on upright stems.
BLOOM: Summer

ALPINE CLOVER
Trifolium dasyphyllum
Pea Family (Fabaceae)

Red/Pink Flowers

LIFE ZONE: Subalpine, alpine
HABITAT: Open high meadows, rocky soil, tundra
HEIGHT: 1" - 6"
LOOK FOR: Grows in clumps. Leaves divided into three parts, often folded, stiff hairs on margins. Flower clusters of five to twenty heads are bicolored from deep-rose, white or very pale pink on leafless, hairy stems. Narrow and pointed sepals.
BLOOM: Summer

DWARF CLOVER
Trifolium nanum
Pea Family (Fabaceae)

Red/Pink Flowers

LIFE ZONE: Alpine
HABITAT: Tundra slopes, ridges
HEIGHT: 1" - 3"
LOOK FOR: Three parted leaves, slightly toothed, hugging the ground forming dense mats. Few small flower clusters varying in colors, white-pink-deep lavender.
BLOOM: Summer

Red/Pink Flowers

PARRY'S CLOVER
Trifolium parryi
Pea Family (Fabaceae)

LIFE ZONE: Subalpine, alpine
HABITAT: Open high sunny meadows, moist rocky soil, tundra
HEIGHT: 1" - 4"
LOOK FOR: Basal leaves, divided into three leaflets, entire or slightly toothed. Flowering stems are leafless. Flower head rest above leaves with keel, banner, wings varying in colors, pink, purple, deep rose.
BLOOM: Mid-summer

ALPINE LAUREL
Kalmia microphylla
Heath Family (Ericaceae)

Red/Pink Flowers

LIFE ZONE: Subalpine, alpine
HABITAT: Moist meadows, bogs, along streams, lake banks
HEIGHT: 2" - 18"
LOOK FOR: Low, woody shrub-like plant spreading along the ground and/or rocks. Evergreen, lance-shaped leaves hairy underneath and opposite on stem. Clusters of intense pink cup-shaped flowers with five petals and numerous stamens.
BLOOM: Mid-summer

FITWEED
(CASE'S CORYDALIS)
Corydalis caseana
Fumitory Family
(Fumariaceae)

Red/Pink Flowers

LIFE ZONE: Montane, subalpine
HABITAT: Moist, high meadows, open forest
HEIGHT: 2' - 6'
LOOK FOR: Pinnate leaves, alternate on thick stems. Fifty to over hundred white-pinkish-red flowers with spurred petals growing on spike. Grows in dense masses.
BLOOM: Summer

PYGMY BITTERROOT
(ALPINE LEWSIA)
Lewisia pygmaea
Miner's Lettuce Family (Montiaceae)

LIFE ZONE: Subalpine, alpine
HABITAT: Open meadows, rocky slopes, tundra
HEIGHT: 1" - 2"
LOOK FOR: Slender linear basal leaves curving upward. Flower petals with pointed tips ranging in color from magenta, light pink or white. One flower on a minute stem.
BLOOM: Summer

Red/Pink Flowers

114 ROCKY MOUNTAIN ALPINE WILDFLOWERS

Red/Pink Flowers

HORNEMANN'S WILLOWHERB
Epilobium hornemannii
Evening Primrose Family
(Onagraceae)

LIFE ZONE: Montane, subalpine, alpine
HABITAT: Moist areas, along streams, moist meadows
HEIGHT: 4" - 12"
LOOK FOR: Lanceolate leaves widest at the base, opposite on stem, may have reddish stems forming clumps. Tiny pink, pale purple or white flowers with four petals notched on ends.
Bloom: Early summer-autumn

ALPINE LOUSEWORT
(SUDETIC LOUSEWORT)
Pedicularis sudetica ssp. *scopulorum*
Synonym: *Pedicularis scopulorum*
Broomrape Family (Orobanchaceae)

Red/Pink Flowers

LIFE ZONE: Subalpine, alpine
HABITAT: Moist high meadows, rocky areas
HEIGHT: 4" – 8"
LOOK FOR: Leaves deeply dissected and lobed. Deep-rosy pink flowers "beaked" on spike-like stem, covered with woolly cobwebby hairs. Uncommon alpine plant.
BLOOM: Mid-summer

ELEPHANT'S HEAD
Pedicularis groenlandica
Broomrape Family
(Orobanchaceae)

Red/Pink Flowers

LIFE ZONE: Montane, subalpine, alpine
HABITAT: Moist meadows, bogs
HEIGHT: 4" - 24"
LOOK FOR: Basal and stem leaves pinnately divided, fern-like. Deep pink-purplish flowers that are 2 lipped resembling elephant heads. These unique flowers form dense spikes on reddish stems. Rarely white.
BLOOM: Summer

Red/Pink Flowers

SPLIT-LEAF INDIAN PAINTBRUSH
(ROSY PAINTBRUSH)

Castilleja rhexiifolia
Broomrape Family
(Orobanchaceae)

LIFE ZONE: Subalpine, alpine
HABITAT: Forest edges, moist meadows
HEIGHT: 4" - 12"
LOOK FOR: Leaves narrow, three veined and maybe slightly lobed, alternate on stem. Flowers (sepals and bracts) are covered with fine hairs and vary color from rosy pink to magenta. Flower petals are a fused tube, green-yellowish.
BLOOM: Summer

Red/Pink Flowers

LIFE ZONE: Montane, subalpine, alpine
HABITAT: Moist open areas, high meadows
HEIGHT: 1' - 3'
LOOK FOR: Stout plant growing in masses. Upright large, long, broad basal leaves, alternate on stem. Flowers reddish, green, yellowish on spikes. Seed pods reddish.
BLOOM: Summer

DENSE-FLOWERED DOCK
(ALPINE DOCK)
Rumex densiflorus
Buckwheat Family
(Polygonaceae)

ROCKY MOUNTAIN ALPINE WILDFLOWERS

ALPINE PRIMROSE
(FAIRY PRIMROSE)
Primula angustifolia
Primrose Family (Primulaceae)

Red/Pink Flowers

LIFE ZONE: Subalpine, alpine
HABITAT: Rocky slopes, rock outcroppings, tundra
HEIGHT: ½" - 4"
LOOK FOR: Clumps of narrow linear leaves. Vivid deep pink-purple flowers have five petals that are notched on the ends, deep yellow centers. Fragrant.
BLOOM: Summer

Red/Pink Flowers

PARRY'S PRIMROSE
Primula parryi
Primrose Family
(Primulaceae)

LIFE ZONE: Subalpine, alpine
HABITAT: Wet areas, streamsides
HEIGHT: 5" - 16"
LOOK FOR: Long, upright, oblong basal leaves. Three-twelve magenta flowers on stem. Five petals with bright yellow centers on a leafless stalk.
BLOOM: Summer

JAMES' FALSE SAXIFRAGE
(ROCK SAXIFRAGE)
Telesonix jamesii
Saxifrage Family
(Saxifragaceae)

Red/Pink Flowers

LIFE ZONE: Montane, subalpine, alpine
HABITAT: Rock crevices, granite rock outcroppings
HEIGHT: 4" - 20"
LOOK FOR: Basal rosette of rounded leaves with rounded lobes, teeth on margins, alternate on stem. Five rounded deep-pink-violet-magenta flower petals. Endemic to Colorado.
BLOOM: Mid-summer

Blue • Purple Flowers

Sky pilot.

PINNATE-LEAF DAISY
Erigeron pinnatisectus
Sunflower Family (Asteraceae)

LIFE ZONE: Subalpine, alpine
HABITAT: Dry, rocky ground, tundra slopes
HEIGHT: 2" - 5"
LOOK FOR: Pinnately lobed leaves finely dissected. Solitary flowers on stems with blue-purple ray flowers and yellow disks flowers that turn orange-brown with age. Grows in clumps. Phyllaries are hairy.
BLOOM: Mid-summer

Blue/Purple Flowers

ALPINE BLUEBELLS
Mertensia alpina
Borage Family (Boraginaceae)

Blue/Purple Flowers

LIFE ZONE: Alpine
HABITAT: Open sunny tundra slopes, meadows
HEIGHT: 2" - 8"
LOOK FOR: Basal leaves lanceolate, hairy on top, few stem leaves. Clusters of small sky-blue-deep blue tubular (bell-shaped) flowers near top of stem.
BLOOM: Summer

ALPINE FORGET-ME-NOT
Eritrichium nanum
Borage Family (Boraginaceae)

Blue/Purple Flowers

LIFE ZONE: Alpine
HABITAT: Open, sunny tundra slopes, rock outcroppings, gravelly soil
HEIGHT: ½" - 2"
LOOK FOR: Oblong basal leaves with thick silvery hairs forming ground hugging mats. Five petals of sky-blue-deep blue tiny flowers with yellow centers clustered together. Occasionally presents with bright white flowers.
BLOOM: Summer

ROCKY MOUNTAIN ALPINE WILDFLOWERS

PURPLE FRINGE
(SILKY PHACELIA)
Phacelia sericea
Borage Family (Boraginaceae)

LIFE ZONE: Montane, subalpine, alpine
HABITAT: Gravelly slopes, open rocky meadows
HEIGHT: 4" - 12"
LOOK FOR: Leaves lance-shaped, gray-green, pinnately divided, covered with silvery hairs. Dense spikes of deep purple bell-shaped flowers with stamens protruding beyond the petals.
BLOOM: Summer

TALL CHIMING BELLS
(STREAMSIDE BLUEBELLS, FRINGED BLUEBELLS)
Mertensia ciliata
Borage Family (Boraginaceae)

LIFE ZONE: Montane, subalpine, alpine
HABITAT: Moist areas, along streams
HEIGHT: 1' - 4'
LOOK FOR: Lanceolate bluish-green leaves, alternate with several prominent veins. Clusters of blue bell-shaped flowers with five lobes hanging from end of stems.
BLOOM: Summer

ARCTIC BELLFLOWER
(ALPINE HAREBELL)
Campanula uniflora
Bellflower Family (Campanulaceae)

Blue/Purple Flowers

LIFE ZONE: Subalpine, alpine
HABITAT: Dry, rocky tundra meadows, rocky slopes
HEIGHT: 2" - 4"
LOOK FOR: Narrow basal leaves, few alternate stem leaves. Single blue bell-shaped flower with pointed petals on erect stem, and five pointed hairy sepals.
BLOOM: Mid-summer

FRINGED GENTIAN
Gentianopsis thermalis
Synonym: *Gentianopsis detonsa*
Gentian Family (Gentianaceae)

Blue/Purple Flowers

LIFE ZONE: Subalpine, alpine
HABITAT: Moist areas, open meadows, near streams
HEIGHT: 6" - 16"
LOOK FOR: Linear leaves opposite, smooth. Deep-blue-purple single tubular flower, four fringed/scalloped edges, twisted lobes with white centers.
BLOOM: Late summer-autumn

LIFE ZONE: Subalpine, alpine
HABITAT: Moist areas, meadows, tundra slopes
HEIGHT: 2" - 14"
LOOK FOR: Lance-shaped leaves, opposite, smooth. Tiny lavender (rarely white) tubular flowers with pointed petals and heavily fringed throats.
BLOOM: Mid-summer-autumn

LITTLE GENTIAN
(NORTHERN GENTIAN, AUTUMN DWARF GENTIAN)
Gentianella amarella Synonym: *Gentianella acuta*
Gentian Family (Gentianaceae)

Blue/Purple Flowers

ROCKY MOUNTAIN ALPINE WILDFLOWERS

MOSS GENTIAN
(PYGMY GENTIAN)
Gentiana prostrata
Gentian Family
(Gentianaceae)

LIFE ZONE: Alpine
HABITAT: Moist areas in the alpine
HEIGHT: ½" - 4"
LOOK FOR: Leaves smooth, opposite. Tiny blue-purplish tubular flower with four triangular-shaped petals. Flowers quickly close when shaded or touched.
BLOOM: Mid-summer-autumn

Blue/Purple Flowers

PARRY'S GENTIAN
Gentiana parryi
Gentian Family
(Gentianaceae)

LIFE ZONE: Subalpine, alpine
HABITAT: Open meadows, tundra slopes
HEIGHT: 5" - 18"
LOOK FOR: Leaves oval shaped, smooth, opposite on stem. Deep-blue tubular flowers with green bands and spots on the inside of petals.
BLOOM: Late summer-autumn

Blue/Purple Flowers

PERENNIAL FRINGED GENTIAN
Gentianopsis barbellata
Gentian Family (Gentianaceae)

Blue/Purple Flowers

LIFE ZONE: Subalpine, alpine
HABITAT: Rocky, grassy slopes, tundra
HEIGHT: 1" - 6"
LOOK FOR: Mostly basal leaves, thick and spoon-shaped. Tubular light purple-blue flower with four twisted lobes finely fringed on edges.
BLOOM: Summer

Blue/Purple Flowers

STAR GENTIAN
Swertia perennis
Gentian Family
(Gentianaceae)

LIFE ZONE: Subalpine, alpine
HABITAT: Moist open meadows and slopes
HEIGHT: 4" - 20"
LOOK FOR: Long basal leaves, stem leaves opposite. Star-shaped dusty-purple flowers elongated on stems. Five petals and five protruding dark stamens.
BLOOM: Summer

ALPINE KITTENTAIL
Besseya alpine
Plantain Family
(Plantaginaceae)

LIFE ZONE: Subalpine, alpine
HABITAT: Rocky scree slopes, rocky ridges, tundra
HEIGHT: 2" - 8"
LOOK FOR: Hairy, upright, rounded leaves, toothed on margins. Purple-flowers in a spike usually surrounded with white woolly hairs.
BLOOM: Summer

AMERICAN ALPINE SPEEDWELL
Veronica wormskjoldii
Synonym: *Veronica nutans*
Plantain Family (Plantaginaceae)

LIFE ZONE: Subalpine, alpine
HABITAT: Moist areas, along streams
HEIGHT: 3" - 14"
LOOK FOR: Lance-shaped, opposite, hairy leaves. Clusters of tiny deep blue flowers on a hairy slender stem.
BLOOM: Mid-summer-autumn

Blue/Purple Flowers

CLUSTERED PENSTEMON
(PINCUSHION BEARDTONGUE)
Penstemon procerus
Plantain Family (Plantaginaceae)

Blue/Purple Flowers

LIFE ZONE: Montane, subalpine, alpine
HABITAT: Open meadows, moist areas
HEIGHT: 2' - 16"
LOOK FOR: Leaves opposite, smooth. Bright blue-purple tubular flowers densely clustered in spaced whorls on stem.
BLOOM: Mid-late summer

HALL'S BEARDTONGUE
Penstemon hallii
Plantain Family
(Plantiginaceae)

LIFE ZONE: Alpine
HABITAT: Alpine meadows, scree slopes, gravelly soil
HEIGHT: 3" - 8"
LOOK FOR: Basal Leaves linear, narrow, few stem leaves. Brilliant deep blue-violet- purple tubular flowers, streaks in throat. Endemic to Colorado
BLOOM: Summer

Blue/Purple Flowers

ROCKY MOUNTAIN ALPINE WILDFLOWERS

WHIPPLE'S PENSTEMON
Penstemon whippleanus
Plantain Family
(Plantaginaceae)

Blue/Purple Flowers

LIFE ZONE: Subalpine, alpine
HABITAT: Rocky soil, open high meadows, tundra slopes
HEIGHT: 4" - 24"
LOOK FOR: Opposite leaves, widest at the base, usually smooth or slightly toothed. Deep purple-maroon or cream colored tubular flowers, hairy with three-lobed bottom lip and two lobed upper lip on a hairy stem.
BLOOM: Summer

JACOB'S LADDER
Polemonium pulcherrimum
Phlox Family (Polemoniaceae)

LIFE ZONE: Montane, subalpine, alpine
HABITAT: Moist shady areas
HEIGHT: 6" - 12"
LOOK FOR: Leaves alternate, pinnately divided (fern-like). Five small rounded petals pale-blue-lavender with yellow centers.
BLOOM: Summer

SKY PILOT
Polemonium viscosum
Phlox Family
(Polemoniaceae)

LIFE ZONE: Alpine
HABITAT: Rocky, sandy soil, tundra slopes
HEIGHT: 3" - 16"
LOOK FOR: Leaves mostly basal, pinnately divided, hairy. Deep blue-purplish funnel-shaped flowers, stamens with orange anthers on a hairy, sticky stem. Skunk-like aroma.
BLOOM: Summer

ALPINE COLUMBINE
(DWARF COLUMBINE, ROCKY MOUNTAIN BLUE COLUMBINE)
Aquilegia saximontana
Buttercup Family (Ranunculaceae)

Blue/Purple Flowers

LIFE ZONE: Alpine
HABITAT: Alpine scree slopes, around and under boulders, sun or shade
HEIGHT: 2" - 4"
LOOK FOR: Leaves divided into three leaflets. Small blue and white flowers with hooked spurs in the back. Usually nodding on the stems. Endemic to Colorado.
BLOOM: Summer

COLORADO BLUE COLUMBINE
Aquilegia coerulea
Buttercup Family (Ranunculaceae)

Blue/Purple Flowers

LIFE ZONE: Montane, subalpine, alpine
HABITAT: Moist areas, forest, meadows, rocky slopes
HEIGHT: 8" - 3'
LOOK FOR: Leaves divided into rounded lobes. Five white rounded petals with long blue spurs. Five lance-shaped pointed sepals, usually blue, many yellow stamens. Colorado's state flower.
BLOOM: Summer

COLUMBIAN MONKSHOOD
Aconitum columbianum
Buttercup Family (Ranunculaceae)

LIFE ZONE: Subalpine
HABITAT: Moist areas, forest, open meadows
HEIGHT: 2' - 5'
LOOK FOR: Alternate, deeply cut palmately divided leaves on tall sturdy stalk. The deep purple flowers (rarely white) are sepals with upper sepal forming a hood with two side sepals and two lower sepals.
BLOOM: Mid-summer-autumn

Blue/Purple Flowers

ROCKY MOUNTAIN ALPINE WILDFLOWERS

SUBALPINE LARKSPUR
Delphinium barbeyi
Buttercup Family (Ranunculaceae)

LIFE ZONE: Subalpine, alpine
HABITAT: Moist meadows, along streams
HEIGHT: 3' - 6'
LOOK FOR: Alternate leaves deeply palmately divided, toothed. Dark purple-dark blue sepals with spur in back and four-five smaller inner petals, upper petals trimmed white and hairless. Stems are sticky and hairy.
BLOOM: Summer

MOUNTAIN BLUE VIOLET
(HOOK-SPURRED VIOLET)
Viola adunca
Violet Family (Violaceae)

LIFE ZONE: Montane, subalpine, alpine
HABITAT: Moist areas, edges of forest
HEIGHT: 2" - 4"
LOOK FOR: Leaves round-oval shaped hairy, lightly toothed. Dark blue-purplish flower with 2 upper petals, 3 lower petals, white throat streaked with dark lines, back spur. Lower petals hairy.
BLOOM: Spring-summer

Blue/Purple Flowers

Glossary

Alternate: Leaves staggered on each side of stem from different nodes
Anther: Pollen bearing part of the stamen
Banner: Upper petal of a flower, mostly in the pea family
Basal: Leaves at the plant base
Bract: Modified leaf that covers the base of flower petals, protects buds
Bulblet: A small bulb (s) borne above ground, usually in leaf axil or stems
Catkins: A flower structure consisting of a dense spike as in the Willow Family
Clasping: Leaves that wrap around the stem
Cluster: Grouping of individual flowers
Compound leaf: A single leaf with two or more parts (leaflets)
Dioecious: Male and female flowers are found on separate plants
Disk flowers: In the Sunflower Family the center holding tubular flowers
Dissected: Leaves deeply cut into numerous narrow segments
Disturbed: Habitats that are changed by human/natural activity
Drupe: A fleshy fruit with a stony seed
Elongated: Extended out
Endemic: Particular to a specific geographic location
Entire: Leaf edges smooth, not toothed or notched
Filament: Stalk of the stamen supporting the anther
Genus: Name for several species within a Family; first part in the scientific name
Glabrous: Smooth, hairless
Glandular: Having gland (s) on surface, gland-like (sticky)
Hood: An upper petal or sepal forming a cover
Hybridize: The crossing of plants from different species or genera
Keel: Two petals fused together, mostly found in the Pea Family
Lanceolate: A leaf shape that tapers at the end, widest below the middle, spear-like
Leaflet: One part of a compound leaf

Linear: Leaf shape that is straight, long and narrow
Lobe: A rounded leaf or petal segment
Margin: The edges of leaves or petals
Mat: Cushion-like on the ground
Monocarpic: Flowering once and then dying
Node: The point where leaves originate on the stem
Oblong: Leaf shape, rounded longer than wide
Opposite: Leaves positioned across from each other at the same node
Oval: Leaf shape, wider than the length
Ovary: Area where seed develops, part of pistil
Palmate: Leaf arrangement, spreading like fingers on a hand
Palmately compound: Leaf blade divided into separate leaflets originating from the same point
Panicle: repeatedly branched flower clusters with stalked flowers
Petal: Individual piece of a flower
Pinnate: Leaf structure, feather-like
Pinnately compound: Leaf blade divided into separate feather-like leaflets
Pistil: Female reproductive organ of a flower consisting stigma, style and ovary
Phyllaries: Modified leaves that cover the base of flowers in the Sunflower Family. Called bracts in other flower families
Raceme: Flower structure, elongated and unbranched, flowers on stalk from stem
Ray flowers: A characteristic of the Sunflower Family: Strap-like flower petals
Rosette: Ground level dense circular cluster of leaves
Runners: Slender, long trailing stems
Sepals: Segments of the outer flower, usually green but can be indistinguishable from petals
Serrate: Leaf margins with sharp teeth pointing forward
Sessile: Attached directly without a supporting stalk or stem
Smooth: Even surface on leaf margins
Spike: Flower structure unbranched, elongated, flowers attached directly to stem
Spur: An appendage of a petal, usually in the back

Stamen: Male reproductive part of flower consisting of anther and filament
Staminode: Non-functional stamen, produces no pollen
Stellate: Star-shaped hairs
Stigma: Part of the pistil which collects pollen, top of the style
Style: Part of the pistil, tube-like connecting the ovary to the stigma
Tepals: Petals and sepals that is not differentiated from each other, common in the Lily Family
Tubular: Flower shape, tube-like
Veins: Thread of vascular tissue running through flower petals and leaves
Umbel: Flower structure, umbrella-like
Whorled: Leaf structure attached ring-like from a common point on the stem
Wing: Two side petals, usually in the Pea Family

References And Resources

Ackerfield, Jennifer, *Flora of Colorado*, Fort Worth, TX, BRIT Press, 2015.

Beidleman, Linda H., Richard G. Beidleman and Beatrice E. Willard, *Plants of Rocky Mountain National Park*, Rocky Mountain Nature Association and Falcon Press, 2000.

Colorado Native Plant Society: conps.org.

Colorado State University Extension Office: conativeplantmaster.org

Descr. adapted from Ipomopsis globularis (Hoosier Pass ipomopsis): A Technical Conservation Assessment by Susan Spackman Panjabi and David G. Anderson. Reference.com

Flora of North America: efloras.org

Harris, James and Melinda Woolf Harris, *Plant Identification Terminology*, Second Edition, Spring Lake Publishing Spring Lake, Utah, 2001.

Kartesz, J.T., *The Biota of North America Program* (BONAP). 2015. Taxonomic Data Center (bonap.net/tdc). Chapel Hill, N.C.

Marx, Ernie: easterncoloradowildflowers.com

Rocky Mountain Conservancy: rmconservancy.org

Schneider, Al.: swcoloradowildflowers.com

Zwinger H. Ann and Willard E. Beatrice, *Land Above the Trees*, 1972, Harper & Row, Publishers, Inc.

INDEX

White/cream/green Flowers

Achillea millefolium 21
Alp-lily 30
Alpine bistort 41
Alpine dusty maiden 17
Alpine mountain sorrel 42
Alpine phlox 38
Alpine sandwort 24
Alpine spring beauty 23
Alpine thistle 18
Alpine willow 51
Amemone narcissiflora 49
American bistort 43
American false candytuft 22
Androsace chamaejasme 46
Androsace septentrionalis 45
Angelica grayi 16
Anticlea elegans 31
Arctic gentian 29
Bistorta bistortoides 43
Bistorta vivipara 41
Blackhead daisy 19
Brandegee's sky pilot 39
Caltha leptosepala 48
Cerastium arvense 27
Chaenactis douglasii var. *alpine* 17
Chionophila jamesii 37
Cilaria austromontana 53
Cirsium scopulorum 18
Claytonia megarhiza 32
Coulter's daisy 20
Dotted saxifrage 53
Dryas octopetala 50
Eremogone fendleri 25
Erigeron coulteri 20
Erigeron melanocephalus 19
Eriogonum umbellatum var. *majus* 44
Fendler's sandwort 25

Fringed grass-of-parnassus 36
Front range alumroot 54
Gentiana algida. 29
Globe gilia 40
Globeflower. 47
Gray's angelica. 16
Heuchera bracteata 56
Heuchera hallii 54
Hooded lady's tresses 33
Ipomopsis globularis 40
Limnorchis dilatata 34
Lloydia serotina. 30
Long-stalked starwort 26
Marsh marigold. 48
Micranthes rhomboidea 58
Minuartia obtusiloba 24
Mitella stauropetala 57
Mountain death camas 31
Mountain dryad 50
Mouse-ear chickweed. 27
Narcissus anemone 49
Nocceae fendleri 23
Nodding saxifrage 55
Oxyria digyna. 42
Parnassia fimbriata 36
Paronychia pulvinata 28
Parry's lousewort. 35
Pedicularis parryi 35
Phlox condensate 38
Platanthera dilatata. 34
Polemonium brandegeei 39
Pygmy-flower rock jasmine 45
Rock jasmine 46
Rocky mountain alumroot 56
Rocky mountain nailwort. 28
Salix nivalis. 52
Salix petrophila 51
Salix reticulate. 52
Saxifraga austromontana 53
Saxifraga cernua 55

Saxifraga rivularis	59
Sharpleaf valerian	60
Side-flowered mitrewort	57
Smelowskia Americana	22
Snow willow	52
Snowball saxifrage	58
Snowlover	37
Spiranthes romanzoffiana	33
Stellaria longipes	26
Subalpine sulfur flower	44
Trollius albiflorus	47
Valeriana acutiloba	60
Weak saxifrage	59
White bog orchid	34
Wild candytuft	23
Yarrow	21
Zigadenus elegans	31

Yellow / Orange

Agoseris aurantiaca	74
Agoseris glauca	75
Alpine avens	96
Alpine golden buckwheat	92
Alpine ivesia	97
Alpine paintbrush	87
Alpine parsley	62
Alpine poppy	90
Alpine sagewort	63
Alpine twinpod	81
Alpine wallflower	82
Arctic yellow violet	102
Arnica latifolia	66
Arnica parryi	76
Arrowleaf ragwort	64
Artemisia scopulorum	63
Avalanche lily	86
Black-tip ragwort	65
Broadleaf arnica	66
Castilleja occidentalis	89
Castilleja puberula	87
Colorado ragwort	67

Cymopterus alpinus	62
Draba aurea	83
Draba crassa	84
Dwarf mountain ragwort	68
Eriogonum flavum	92
Erysimum capitatum	82
Erythronium grandiflorum	86
Eschscholtz's buttercup	93
Fern leaf lousewort	88
Geum rossii	96
Golden draba	83
Golden saxifrage	99
Heuhera parvifolia	100
Hoary groundsel	69
Holm's ragwort	70
Hymenoxys grandiflora	73
Hymenoyxs acaulis	80
Ivesia gordonii	97
Ligularia bigelovii	72
Ligularia soldanella	67
Little-leaf alumroot	100
Mimulus tilingii	91
Mt. Albert goldenrod	71
Nodding ragwort	72
Old man of the mountain	73
Orange agoseris	74
Oreoxis alpina	62
Packera crocata	78
Packera werneriifolia	69
Pale agoseris	75
Papaver radicatum ssp. *Kluanensis*	90
Parry's arnica	76
Pedicularis bracteosa	88
Physaria alpina	81
Pygmy goldenweed	77
Ranunculus adoneus	95
Ranunculus eschscholtzii	93
Ranunculus macauleyi	94
Rocky mountain buttercup	94
Saffron ragwort	78

Saxifraga chrysantha	99
Saxifraga flagellaris	101
Sedum lanceolatum	85
Senecio amplectens var. *amplectens*	79
Senecio amplectens var. *holmii*	70
Senecio atratus	65
Senecio bigelovii	72
Senecio fremontii var. *blitoides*	68
Senecio soldanella	67
Senecio triangularis	64
Showy alpine ragwort	79
Sibbaldia	98
Sibbaldia procumbens	98
Snow buttercup	95
Solidago simplex	71
Stemless four-nerve daisy	80
Subalpine monkeyflower	91
Tetraneuris acaulis var. *caespitosa*	80
Thick draba	84
Tonestus pygmaeus	77
Viola biflora	102
Western yellow paintbrush	89
Whiplash saxifrage	101
Yellow stonecrop	85

Red / Pink

Alpine clover	109
Alpine laurel	112
Alpine lousewort	116
Alpine primrose	120
Castilleja rhexiifolia	118
Corydalis caseana	113
Dense-flowered dock	119
Dwarf clover	110
Elephant's head	117
Epilobium hornemannii	115
Erigeron elatior	105
Erigeron glacialis	104
Erigeron peregrinus	104
Fitweed	113
Glacier daisy	104

Hornemann's willowherb	115
James' false saxifrage	122
Kalmia microphylla	112
King's crown	107
Lewisia pygmaea	114
Moss campion	106
Parry's clover	111
Parry's primrose	121
Pedicularis groenlandica	117
Pedicularis scopulorum	116
Pedicularis sudetica ssp. *Scopulorum*	116
Primula angustifolia	120
Primula parryi	121
Pygmy bitterroot	104
Queen's crown	108
Rhodiola integrifolia	107
Rhodiola rhodantha	108
Rumex densiflorus	119
Silene acaulis	106
Split-leaf Indian paintbrush	118
Tall daisy	105
Telesonix jamesii	122
Trifolium dasyphyllum	109
Trifolium nanum	110
Trifolium parryi	111

Blue / Purple

Aconitum columbianum	145
Alpine bluebells	125
Alpine columbine	143
Alpine forget-me-not	126
Alpine kittentail	136
American alpine speedwell	137
Aquilegia coerulea	144
Aquilegia saximontana	143
Arctic bellflower	129
Besseya alpina	136
Campanula uniflora	129
Clustered penstemon	138
Colorado blue columbine	144
Columbian monkshood	145

Delphinium barbeyi	146
Erigeron pinnatisectus	124
Eritrichium nanum	126
Fringed gentian	130
Gentianella acuta	131
Gentianella amarella	131
Gentiana parryi	133
Gentiana prostrate	132
Gentianopsis barbellata	134
Gentianopsis detonsa	130
Gentianopsis thermalis	130
Hall's beardtongue	139
Jacob's ladder	141
Little gentian	131
Mertensia alpina	125
Mertensia ciliata	127
Moss gentian	132
Mountain blue violet	147
Parry's gentian	133
Penstemon hallii	139
Penstemon procerus	138
Penstemon whippleanus	140
Perennial fringed gentian	134
Phacelia sericea	127
Pinnate-leaf daisy	124
Polemonium pulcherrimum	141
Polemonium viscosum	142
Purple fringe	127
Sky pilot	142
Star gentian	135
Subalpine larkspur	146
Swertia perennis	135
Tall chiming bells	128
Veronica nutans	137
Veronica wormskjoldii	137
Viola adunca	147
Whipple's penstemon	140

About the Author

Marlene has been photographing Colorado's wildflowers while on her hiking and climbing adventures since 1974. She soon developed a deep interest to learn more about the botany behind their beautiful faces. She has participated in informal and formal studies and extensive fieldwork to further her knowledge and understanding of Colorado's rich and diverse flora. She has earned her Native Plant Master Certification.

Marlene has climbed Colorado's 54 14ers, the 126 USGS named peaks in Rocky Mountain National Park and 43 State High Points. She has been a member of the Colorado Mountain Club since 1979 and is a member of the Colorado Native Plant Society. She teaches wildflower classes for the Rocky Mountain Conservancy and provides community programs that educate and promote stewardship for Colorado's wildflowers.

Marlene holds a Masters Degree in Social Work and is a Certified Addiction Counselor. She guides in Rocky Mountain National Park and enjoys sharing the scenery as well as her knowledge of the plant life and habitats the park has to offer. She is the author of *The Best Front Range Wildflower Hikes* and *Rocky Mountain Wildflowers*, 2nd edition, published by CMC Press.

Join Today.
Adventure Tomorrow

The Colorado Mountain Club helps you maximize living in an outdoor playground and connects you with other adventure-loving mountaineers. We summit 14ers, climb rock faces, work to protect the mountain experience and educate generations of Coloradans.

Visit cmc.org/readerspecials for great membership offers to our valued read